YOU
CAN NEVER
GO WRONG
BY LYING

YOU CAN NEVER GO WRONG BY LYING

and Other Solutions to the Moral and Social Dilemmas of Our Time

PATRICIA MARX

Illustrations by Jim Carson

HOUGHTON MIFFLIN COMPANY
Boston   1985

To my grandmother

Library of Congress Cataloging-in-Publication Data

Marx, Patricia.
You can never go wrong by lying.

I. Title.
PN6162.M275 1985   818′.5402   85-17533
ISBN 0-395-38465-6

Printed in the United States of America

S 10 9 8 7 6 5 4 3 2 1

Contents

Acknowledgments

I'd like to thank Douglas McGrath, Mark O'Donnell, Sarah and Charlie Stuart, my family, my editor Frances Tenenbaum, and my agent Esther Newberg.

Chapter 1

Kids

Do you have to let little children beat you at games?

It is important to the development of a child's ego that he be a winner once in a while. Otherwise, he will never have confidence, will not be able to find love or hold a job, and will end up in the gutter, adding to the burden of the welfare state. But any Tom, Dick, or Harry can teach the child confidence. One presumes there is an uncle or some stooge-for-hire willing to lose a game or two of Parcheesi.

Who, on the other hand, is to teach the child disappointment? Who is qualified to show him that life isn't always fair, and that even the most honest-seeming people don't always play by the rules? Someone must beat it into the child's brain that just because he is a pip-squeak the world is not going to look the other way and give him a break.

Sure, it is warming to see the delight in a triumphant child's eyes. Sure, it is unpleasant to trip someone under three feet just as he reaches the finish line. But you must rise above *your* needs and desires this once and rout your little opponent. Besides, it is very important to your own ego that you be a winner, and the best way to start is by beating a child and working yourself up.

How should you tell the children you have to put the dog to sleep?

You could tell a little white lie: "Well, it's off to college for Sparky!" Or you could be firm, stand straight, and like the Mother in *Old Yeller*, say, "I'll shoot him if you can't, Son, but either way, we've got to do it." Still, the best method is to sit down with the children and explain that Sparky will no longer be with the family, emphasizing at the same time that it is really all for the best: "What lucky little person gets to eat out of Sparky's bowl from now on?"

Do you have to give the adults in your family birthday presents?

No. However, any adopted child should give his new parents birthday presents until it is legally impossible for them to return him.

Are you entitled to cash compensation from your parents if you never had braces as a child?

You are, but don't bring it up. They'll present you with a bill for good-teeth genes.

If you tell a child — whom you thought already knew — that there is no Santa Claus, should you tell the parents what you did?

Why spoil Christmas for them, too? You have done enough damage, although now that the child's innocence has been shattered so traumatically, you might as well go ahead and tell him the rest: how, sometimes, for no reason known to medical science, a person can become paralyzed for life while he is sleeping; and how hundreds of children just like him are kidnapped and tortured every day in Chile on their way home from school; and what happens when parents make a teeny-weeny little mistake, and the IRS has to come and take away the house and the dog and throw everyone into the poor-house.

If your son is hitchhiking through Ireland when another skirmish in Lebanon breaks out, should you worry that he might have taken a side trip to the Mideast?

Yes, if you've finished worrying about the IRA.

How can you tell your teen-age daughter she is dressed like a prostitute?

Parents who are overly critical of an adolescent may prevent that adolescent from growing into an autonomous adult capable of making decisions. On the other hand, one of the ways an adolescent knows her parents care is by the concern they show in her appearance. It is a thin line, therefore, that a parent must walk, but it *is* possible to express interest without making value judgments. Before your daughter leaves, casually ask, "Dear, will the others be wearing cheap and vulgar dresses to the party, too?" or say, "Promise you'll show me sometime how you manage to create such a gaudy effect using only FDA-approved cosmetics."

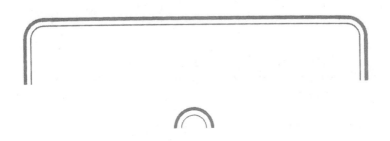

Do you have to punish your child for biting the vile little girl who lives next door?

As moral guardian, you must let your child know that biting is wrong, but there is a way to admonish ambiguously so as to leave the door open for your child to bite the girl again if she ever sets foot near your property. Tell your child what a judge once told a nice man who unfortunately had been charged with grand larceny: "Ordinarily, I'd give you twenty years for this," the judge said, "but you seem to have punished yourself, and that is the worst kind of punishment there is. Run along, now."

What should you do if you are asked to write a college reference for a student you detest?

One of the following recommendations should suffice:

_____ is a very tidy student who has a part in his/her hair that is one of the straightest I have ever seen! He/she sits way in the back of the classroom, and yet, he/she seems to see everything on the board! I hear your school has some pretty big lecture halls and I know _____ will fit right in.

Though _____ steals and cheats, he/she would be a definite asset to your college by broadening the diversity of your student body. His/her large collection of stereos and car radios suggests that he/she might have something to add as well to your school's audio-visual department. And, as _____'s English teacher, I feel strongly he/she will do well in this subject. The enclosed essay is an example of the fine, imaginative prose _____ is capable of writing when on the right drugs. I recommend _____ most highly and would be happy to write an additional reference, if necessary, to the bursar's office with regard to _____'s request for child support and alimony to supplement his student loan.

From the looks of the attendance record, _____ is apparently very involved in extracurricular activities.

8

Chapter 2

Work and Money

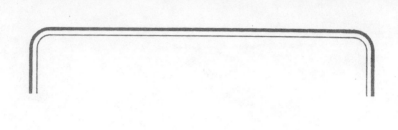

What should you do if your boss propositions you?

Theoretically, there is no problem here. Freud said the well-adjusted person is one who is happy in both love and work, but this could have been just a line Freud used with his female patients.

Freud had many other clever little tricks — like transference — which he used to make women fall in love with him. You should be on guard against these tricks, for if you succumb to Freud's charms and have an affair with him, you will never get better. Tell him you respect his work, especially on dream interpretation, and agree that an affair would be convenient, but that he reminds you of your father, and you are afraid your mother would feel left out. Freud will understand.

If you do not work for Freud, just say no.

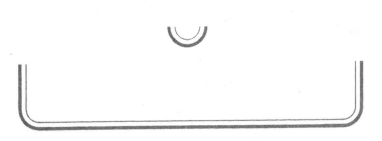

> What happens if you tell yourself that your stock will definitely go up if you can throw the apple core into the wastepaper basket on the first try and then you miss?

Your personal fortunes in the stock market cannot be predicted by throwing an apple core into a wastepaper basket. True, no one knows how the stock market works, but we do know that it is very complicated. If you fail to get the apple core into the wastepaper basket, throw again. Fewer than two out of three tries is not statistically significant.

> If a Brinks truck overturns, spilling millions of dollars onto the highway, may you join the hundreds and hundreds of passers-by who have stopped to grab up the loot?

Two wrongs do not make a right, but hundreds and hundreds do.

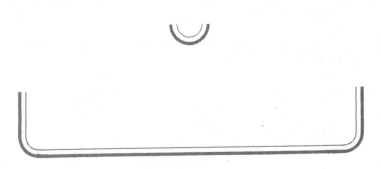

If your boss mispronounces a word in front of you, do you have to mispronounce the same word to be polite?

Manners have nothing to do with it. A language decays when people habitually abuse it. That is what happened to Latin. The Roman slaves, yearning for emancipation, mispronounced words left and right to impress their owners. The language withered and eventually turned into Italian. If you have any pride in your heritage, you will not allow the English language to suffer the same fate. If, however, you would like the company's box seats for the World Series next Saturday, you should mispronounce the word.

If your financial life is very simple because you make no money and have virtually no assets, should you do your own taxes?

You should never do anything you can pay others to do, even if you can't afford it.

What if you are jobless and homeless and can't even get food stamps because you lack the motivation to do anything?

You must make an effort to improve your life. Force yourself to buy a lottery ticket.

Is it okay to steal stationery supplies from the office?

"Steal" is a bad way to put it. Should you "use" pens from work at home? Should you "share" a few with friends and relatives? Yes. According to a study in *Psychology Today*, workers take office supplies as a means of venting their anger toward their boss. Consequently, they are more content and more productive than workers who don't take a thing. It is not just your right to take stationery supplies: It is your duty.

What should you do if you think the house painter is stealing money from you?

Steal his paint.

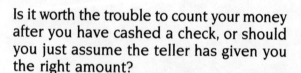

Is it worth the trouble to count your money after you have cashed a check, or should you just assume the teller has given you the right amount?

It would be very insulting to the teller if you were to count your money. The teller trusted you — he did not doubt your signature, he did not call the security guard to frisk you for a weapon. You must act with reciprocal magnanimity. Moreover, while you are waiting in line to cash your check, you should leave your wallet on the counter where they keep the deposit slips. This will display to the other customers your faith in their rectitude.

Should you paint yourself richer than you are to gain the respect of others?

You can never go wrong by lying. Not only will others think more highly of you, but soon you will be asked to join committees and given passes so that you don't have to wait in lines. Your friends, comparing themselves to you, will think they are poorer than they really are, which will make them feel justified when they complain about their hard lives. This is the ploy meteorologists used when they came up with the "windchill factor" to make cold people feel like martyrs.

How do you borrow money from someone you already owe a lot of money to?

Easy. According to Bernardo Grinspun, the former Economics Minister of Argentina who was responsible for arranging the 1.42 billion-dollar loan from the International Monetary Fund, "a friend in need is a friend indeed." In other words, the more money you owe someone, the more interested he will be in cementing your friendship so that you will be sure to repay him someday. To ingratiate himself, he will gladly lend you all the money you want.

Should you take out a mortgage on a house when you know for a fact that you can never meet the payments, even in a million years?

By all means, take out as large a mortgage as you can trick the bank into giving you. Money is no issue when you don't have any.

Chapter 3

Love and Friendship

Is it wrong to borrow your friend's brand-new luggage?

Your friend has brand-new luggage lying around the house because he uses his old luggage when he travels. He does not want his new luggage to become shabby, for then he would have two sets of old luggage. That would be senseless. He might as well have not bought the new luggage.

If you borrow your friend's new luggage, your friend's system will be ruined, and he will lose much sleep figuring out how to remedy it. That is no way to treat a friend. You could borrow your friend's shabby luggage, but then you would be embarrassed in the baggage pickup area. What you should do is borrow your friend's unused luggage, and when you return home, buy him a new set. This is a nice way to say thank you and it makes everyone happy.

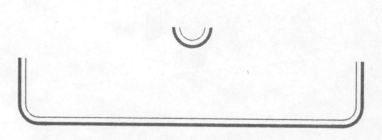

How should you respond to a friend who asks a favor of you on his deathbed when you have no intention of carrying out the favor after his death?

"You'll have to speak up . . . I still can't hear you . . . Pardon? . . . Oh, damn! Nurse, I think my friend is dead."

What can you give a friend who has everything?

Shelves.

What should you do if you are having an extramarital affair and are discovered by your spouse after four months?

You have every reason to be enraged. Tell your spouse it is about time! Anyone so oblivious to your having such a passionate, wonderful, mutually fulfilling affair for four months is clearly insensitive and self-absorbed. That is why you had to have the affair in the first place; and if your spouse was a considerate human being, he would now spare you the tedious ordeal of breaking up with him and just leave. A divorce, you might add, could be for the best. Sociologists now report a high divorce rate, and yet none of your friends seem to be divorced. Someone has to keep the statistics honest, and it might as well be you two who make the sacrifice since all your friends have such happy marriages.

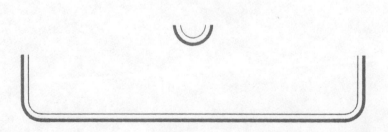

What should you do if you're housesitting for a friend and the tropical fish die?

Put the fish into a Baggie filled with water so they won't wither and take the Baggie to a pet store. Buy some more of the same fish. This will not be too difficult as tropical fish are still fish, and fish look basically alike. On the other hand, if it is a dog you have accidentally killed, your problem is serious. You might have to go to several stores before you find a dog with exactly the same markings. Plus, dogs know tricks so you will have a lot of training to do.

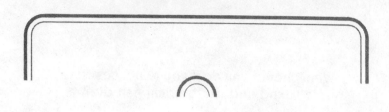

If you have been placing bets through a friend with his bookie whom you have never met, and then your friend dies before paying you the money the bookie owes you, how can you find the bookie?

Go to the funeral dressed as if you were going to the Kentucky Derby—plaid suit, binoculars, tip sheet. As you walk by your dead friend to pay respects, place a horseshoe-shaped wreath over the casket and whisper loudly to the body, "I'll lay you two to one you're only kidding." The bookie will appear before the last strain of the organ. He knows a customer when he sees one.

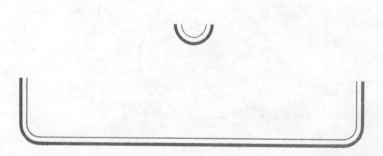

When can you stop worrying that you've forgotten to turn off the iron in your friend's apartment, where you're staying while she is in France?

Most accidents occur within ten miles of the home, so if you are driving along and you have gone ten miles, chances are nothing will happen after that.

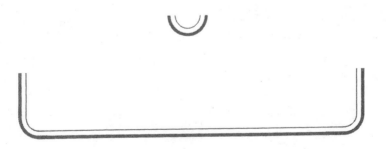

Do you have to love your family?

No, but you must acknowledge the existence of any family member you meet perchance on the street. It is okay to deny being related to a cousin, but you must, even if it is a detriment professionally, admit to your nuclear family (there is no such thing as a "brother once removed"). At home, it's another matter. Hate and love touch each other. You have your choice.

What should you do if you leave a message on a phone answering machine and later regret it?

Have an agent from the FBI leave a message that someone has been impersonating you, and the Bureau would appreciate the tape sent immediately to them for investigation. If you'd rather not enlist the help of others, break into the house and confiscate the tape yourself. The Freedom of Information Act, loosely interpreted, gives you this right.

What can you say when someone says he loves you but the feeling is not mutual?

Point out to him that he is lucky, for if he loves you that much, he has the capacity to love others as well, whereas you may never feel so passionately about someone. Try to restrain the envy in your voice.

Is it pathetic to call someone on a Saturday night?

It may be, but then it is equally pathetic for the person you are calling to be home to pick up the phone. If the reason he is home is because he is throwing a huge party to which you alone are not invited, you do not want to know this person —and evidently vice versa.

How can you get out of a date and make it look like the other person is canceling?

YOU (on phone an hour before date): All set for the darts tournament tonight?

THE DATE: Can't wait.

YOU: Your voice sounds funny, Jane. I hope you're not coming down with that flu that gives you laryngitis for life if you don't get enough rest *as soon as possible.*

JANE: I feel great.

YOU: Did you hear about the prisoner who escaped and is probably stalking the area around the stadium grounds, where we're going tonight?

JANE: How exciting! Maybe we'll get our pictures in the paper.

YOU: Of course, the guy's a sniper, and the odds of his getting us are about twelve in a thousand—maybe a little higher since our seats are right behind the dart boards.

JANE: Oh good, I don't have to bring my glasses.

YOU: But that's where Mother likes to sit, and she's the boss. Would you rather sit next to her or to Father?

JANE: Gosh, I don't care . . .

YOU: You have to wash your hair? That's okay. I'll catch you later.

When good friends go through a bitter divorce, to what extent must you swear allegiance to one?

This problem is akin to the one faced in the Civil War by the parents of brothers who fought brothers. In most cases, these parents tried to support both sons equally, sending cookies to the North and South and putting up whichever army happened to be in town.

Some parents, however, placed their own politics before the welfare of their families. These parents interfered in their sons' quarrels and chose sides. The majority, historians tell us, picked their Confederate sons because the manners down South were genteel and because the region offered more attractive retirement possibilities than the North. The parents who picked their Union sons said they had been disappointed by the quitter attitude displayed by the South when it seceded. Also, the North, it was felt, had much more interesting memorabilia than the South since it was a manufacturing center.

After the war, there was greater tension, especially that first Thanksgiving, in the families where the parents had picked favorites than in those where the parents had remained impartial. So take heed: Move to a neutral state.

Chapter 4

Parties

If a guest unexpectedly brings a Carvel "Fudgie the Whale" ice cream cake to your dinner party, do you have to serve it instead of the dessert you spent three days preparing?

Albert Einstein discovered that energy can be converted into matter. A corollary to Einstein's theory, in dessert terms, is that your guest's cake, which he spent *no energy* making, does *not matter*. Toss it. That is what Albert Einstein would have done, and he was a genius.

Is it fashionable to have a good time or a bad time on New Year's Eve?

As with childhood, it is fashionable to enjoy New Year's Eve and then claim you did not.

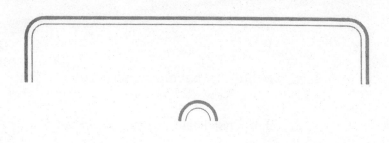

If you're having a dinner party, and a guest asks for decaffeinated coffee, which you don't have, is it all right to serve an inferior brand of real coffee and pretend it is decaf?

You must. Do you want your friend to fall asleep while driving home?

(This does not mean that it is always correct to serve your guests food or drink that is not what it appears to be. Atreus, the legendary Greek, was clearly in the wrong when he killed his brother's sons and then served their flesh to him at a banquet.)

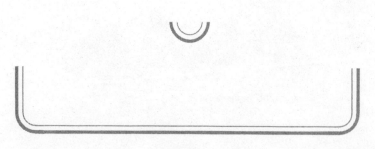

What should you do if someone you don't like invites you to a party you're dying to attend?

Don't go.

Janet Bunten, a bright, attractive, young account executive, said yes when Ken Tripp invited her to a Columbus Day video party after they ran into each other while waiting for a taxi. Janet felt obliged to invite Ken to her office party, and before long, they were married.

Today Janet, divorced from Ken, lives in a cramped apartment with their three children, who don't even have winter coats. Janet has no social life because all their friends like Ken better.

What Janet should have done when Ken invited her to the party was to explain very kindly that, although he seemed nice, at the present time she had all the friends she needed, but that she certainly would notify him immediately if there was a death, and a slot opened up.

What should you do if you meet a celebrity whom you greatly admire at a dinner party?

What I do with celebrities, to prove my deep respect and awe, is snub them. When we are introduced, I don't say, "I have seen you in everything you've done, and I particularly liked you as the girl who came out of the bottle in that Prell commercial," or "Congratulations on that arms negotiations deal." Unctuous flattery like that would make the celebrities think I am buttering them up to get them to autograph my napkin. Instead, I say, "I didn't catch what you do, Your Holiness," or "Cher? Is that some kind of foreign name?"

At dinner, if a celebrity, say Telly Savalas, asks me to pass the applesauce, I look the other way, pretending I did not hear, so that he does not think I am out to get a job for my niece. At the end of the evening, after I have apologized for taking Mrs. Savalas's sable, laughing as I show how much it looks like my fun fur, I can rest assured that someday, if ever I ask Telly for a favor, I will not be considered just another fawning idol.

How should you act if you never received an invitation to a wedding you were orally invited to and then you run into the couple a few days before the event?

Ask them if they ever got your present (that you never sent).

What should you do if you're at a funeral and you can't stop laughing?

Though it is in excellent form to cry at a wedding, by some bizarre logic, it is considered rude to laugh at a funeral, even if the deceased died the way Mama Cass did, with a ham sandwich in her mouth. The survivors of the deceased are hurt, and therefore, you should try as hard as you can not to laugh. This will make you laugh harder and harder until eventually, tears will stream down your cheeks, and everyone will be happy.

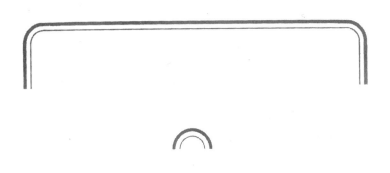

How long do you have to stay at a party to get credit for going?

You have missed the point. Credit is what you get by returning something that you have bought or charged, for instance brandy snifters. In most department stores, the transaction is made by computer and will show up on your next bill.

Unfortunately, this type of business is out of the question in most homes, so you'll have to steal a knickknack, preferably one of great real or sentimental value. A piece of antique jewelry would be nice; a prescription drug will do. Mail whatever you have selected back to your host a few days later, and you'll get all the credit you need.

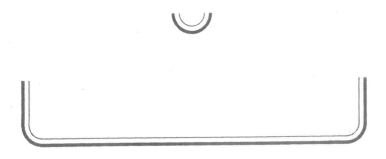

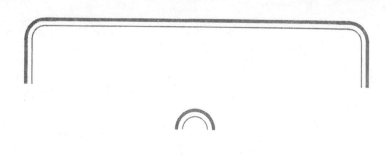

How can you liven up a dull party at your house?

A small grease fire in the kitchen. Calamity draws people to-
gether, and before you know it, the guests will be sharing
lively anecdotes about other fires they've seen. If the fire rages
uncontrollably, don't panic. Firemen are gregarious and tend
to know a lot of good party jokes as well as interesting facts
about fires. (Did you know that in Liverpool fire sirens play
"Let It Be" as a tribute to the Beatles?) The worst that can
happen is that your house burns to the ground, the party
disbands, and your problem is over.

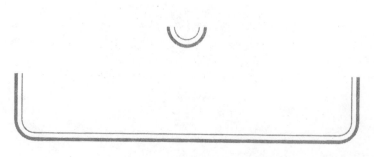

Chapter 5

Literature and the Arts

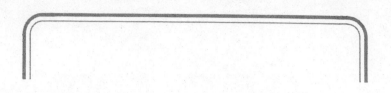

When should you walk out of a movie?

When you realize that your watch is more interesting than the movie.

Does it count to send someone a Christmas card in lieu of a letter you owe?

It counts for Hallmark, not for you.

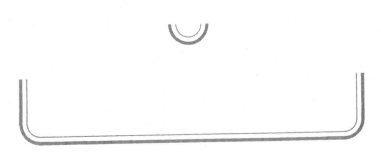

Should you keep on going when you realize halfway through a secret you're telling that the person you're telling it to is the same person who told it to you in confidence?

You are part of a tradition of oral storytellers, of whom Homer is the most famous. For people like you and Homer, retelling is the crucial process by which you perfect your epic poem or, as in your case, the story about your friend's desperate gambling addiction that is tearing asunder his family and business.

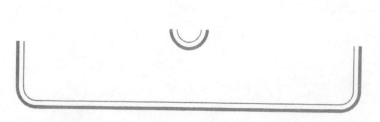

Is it cheating to fast-forward through the commercials of a movie you have taped on the VCR?

It is your right to skip the commercials, but you should be aware of the consequences. As more and more people follow your lead, the value of a commercial will naturally diminish, and Madison Avenue, not to mention the enterprise of television itself, will be left topsy-turvy. This is exactly what Karl Marx meant when he predicted that once the workers took over the means of production the capitalist system would crumble. The choice is yours: If you prefer the TV programs in the Free World to those behind the Iron Curtain, watch the commercials.

Is it worth the time and energy to sharpen
a pencil with a dull point, or should you
just throw it out and use another one?

Indirectly, pencils grow on trees. Throw it out.

Should you feel guilty for not finishing a book you were reading?

Yes, but you should feel more guilty about all those books you never started.

Is it wrong to read a novel you bought for someone else before you wrap it?

Yes, the surprise element is lost when a novel is read for the second time.

Is there a minimum amount of time you must linger before a painting in a museum to prove that you have culture?

The runner who jogs through a forest at great speed is rarely criticized for failing to appreciate nature. Unfortunately, the museum-goer must be more sensitive to his surroundings, but fortunately, it is possible to fake it. What counts is not the speed at which you make your way through the museum but the pacing. If you rush past *Study in Angst* and dwell before *Study in Angst #2* people will think you can tell the difference between Abstract Neo-Expressionism and Neo-Abstract-Expressionism.

If your very heavy TV set breaks, should you take it into the shop or call in a repairman, even though he charges $30 with an additional $25 if nothing is wrong?

If you bring the TV in, there is a chance you will have a heart attack lifting it down the stairs and will have to stay in the hospital for two weeks. This will cost you $12,000, minimum. You can hire someone to help you lift the set. This will cost you $15 an hour. There is always the risk, though, that your helper will have a heart attack, which will cost you the $12,000 on top of the $15, or slightly less if he has the heart attack toward the beginning of the hour; unless he decides to sue you for two million. Two million is a lot. I recommend calling in the TV repairman. But first, heave an axe through your set to ensure that something is really wrong with it, and you won't be throwing $25 down the tube.

What should you do if you find a twenty-year-old library book from your old junior high in your attic?

You own the book by common law. Still, you can't put it on your shelf lest someone not versed in the law think you are a thief, which in fact you are. You can't throw the book away because the garbageman might form a low opinion of you, and you can't burn it because you'd be a bigot. You certainly cannot return it to your old junior high because the principal might look up your record and see that you did not turn in that paper on "The Significance of the Title *Pride and Prejudice*" and take away your diploma. Put the book back where you found it.

If someone takes you to the theater, do you have to pretend to like the production to show your gratitude?

Yes, and the more dreadful the play, the more effusive your gratitude should be, for your friend has poured money down the drain to please you: Nothing is more touching. If there are no positive words to describe the play, remember that it is only a small part of the Theater Experience. Was the chair comfortable?

If you read most of a magazine in line at the grocery store, are you morally obliged to buy it?

Most likely you are reading an article in a self-improvement magazine, let's say "Angela Davis Fifteen Years Later: Fifteen Beauty Tips." If you have not finished the magazine, then by definition you are not yet perfect. You don't have to pretend to be a perfect person and buy the magazine just because it is the right thing to do. It will take you about eighteen years to attain physical, moral, and spiritual perfection, assuming you are an average reader. (The average American, according to a Gallup poll, spends thirty-nine hours a year in line at the store, reading magazines at the rate of five self-improvement articles an hour.) When you are perfect, however, you will have no need to pick up a magazine at the grocery store, so the question of whether you must buy one you've read part of will never arise.

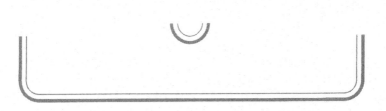

Should you feel gauche when you yell "Bravo!" after the first movement of Beethoven's Fifth because you assumed the loud crescendo to have been the finale?

The appreciation of a piece of music is a subjective matter. Just because your interpretation of where the end of the Fifth falls differs from that of the composer, the conductor, and the entire audience does not mean you are wrong. Indeed, music historians may someday discover the subsequent movements to be spurious ones, tacked on after Beethoven's death to make the symphony more commercial. If the first movement signals the end for you, then get up and leave. You will reach the parking lot first and beat all that traffic.

Chapter 6

Travel

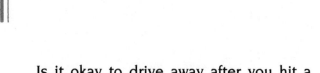

Is it okay to drive away after you hit a parked car, if you have to get to the polls before they close?

Absolutely. This is a democracy, and if everyone took the time to locate the owner of the car and exchange insurance policy numbers with him, no one would vote, and as a consequence, we might have a dictatorship.

Our founding fathers had the foresight to imagine predicaments like the one above. Driving, our laws tell us, is a "privilege" whereas voting is a "right." That is why you must take a test in order to drive, but you only have to sign up to vote. Obviously, it is more important, in the eyes of the law, to vote than to drive. All police officers know this and would therefore applaud your decision to leave the scene of the accident as quickly as possible.

But what if your car was also damaged? Just as you would be entitled to a military funeral if you had been killed in the line of fire during a war, so you are entitled to insurance money if you have damaged your car while carrying out your duties as a citizen on election day. Not all insurance companies agree with this, however.

54

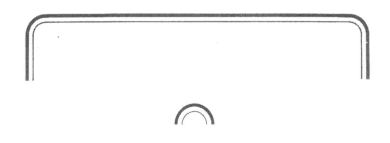

How can you get the cab driver to stop talking to you?

The best way is to use sign language, but if you've already made the mistake of telling the driver — in words — where you want to go, do what a friend of mine did to silence a cab driver who was ranting on and on about the violence in New York and how even if you're being murdered and your neighbor sees you, he won't look etc., etc., etc. "Shit!" said my friend. "There ain't nothin' you can't shoot your way out of!"

Should you be for or against the space program?

The space program promises to explore new frontiers and open new worlds, which seems nosy. Besides, we already have the shuttles between New York and Boston, and New York and Washington, two excellent arenas in which eligible professionals can meet each other; do we really need another? The same money could be used for more humanitarian purposes like programs for the poor. On the other hand, the money not spent on space would also not be spent on the poor. The money would be spent on defense, and nowadays defense includes space, so it is really a waste of time to be against the space program in favor of programs for the poor. A compromise position would be to support programs to help the poor in space. Space is infinite; maybe the poor could be trained to grow ivy there and sell it on Earth. This would have the incidental benefit of beautifying outer space without having to design murals.

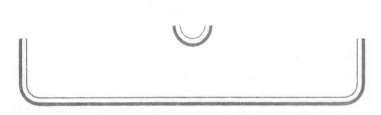

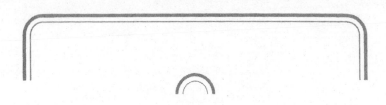

Should you drive on the top deck or the bottom deck of the George Washington Bridge?

Most people drive on the top, believing it is safer to squash than to be squashed. In truth, if the bridge goes, so do you, no matter which deck you are on. A more significant consideration are low-flying meteorites:

Deck	Fatality Risk
Top	.00000000000000000000007
Bottom	.00000000000000000000009

NOTE: The risk of being hit by a *low* low-flying meteorite is greater on the lower deck, but the chance that one of those will hit you on either deck is statistically negligible, so don't worry about it.

Is it worth the trouble to complain about the view from your hotel room if you are staying only one night?

Certainly, the fact that you are staying only one night is not the issue; wouldn't you protest that your lamb chop had a nail in it even if you were going to eat only one chop? In the future, though, lodge complaints *before* you arrive at the hotel. Call the concierge from the airport and tell him your room is not on a high enough floor, the kids next door are making a racket, and there aren't enough towels in the bathroom. Under the laws of probability, you will be right on at least one account. This is known as preventive complaining and will ensure that your stay at the hotel is an agreeable one.

What should you do if you are caught on the turnpike in the middle of miles and miles of bumper-to-bumper traffic and you have an interview in fifteen minutes for a terrific job?

The fear of success is powerful. Obviously, you are so afraid of dealing with the happiness that this job would bring that your subconscious has maneuvered your car into this traffic jam, or perhaps even caused it. You should undergo intensive therapy to get rid of this neurosis, but in the meantime, pull over to the shoulder of the road and step on it. If the shoulder lane is blocked, and you have some sort of hang-up about driving the wrong way on the other side of the turnpike, then at least use your time productively:

1. Come up with a new form of literature that takes less than one hour to read, to replace the dying novel.

2. Figure out a rotating schedule so that the Israelis, Arab states, and the PLO can all share Jerusalem without ever seeing each other.

3. Create a strain of wheat that can be grown on the highway and is resistant to carbon monoxide, so that we can increase our wheat supply and really make the Soviet Union jealous.

If you call American Airlines, and they put you on hold, and you wait forty-five minutes, are you better off hanging up and calling again or staying on the line?

American Airlines is playing hard to get, and the only way you will ever reach them is to pretend you aren't interested. Hang up, book a flight with TWA, then try American. You'll find, I believe, that American Airlines is now whistling a more obsequious tune. After you have reserved a seat with the suddenly available American, perhaps you should reconsider: Is American the kind of airline that will be late? Will you be bumped to make room for another passenger? And who *were* they talking to for so long, anyway? Call American back and tell them you feel you must end the relationship. Knowing American Airlines, they will offer you extra miles in the Advantage Club.

What should you do if you have an accident while driving someone's Jaguar?

Driving someone's cherished car can make one very nervous, and nervous drivers are the most dangerous drivers on the road. This is probably why you had the accident. It is very important for your confidence that you get right back in that Jag and try again.

Should you say anything if you're in the Express Line, and the person in front of you has thirty items, and you have to pick someone up at the airport?

Don't talk. Just eat. You have twenty items to get through.

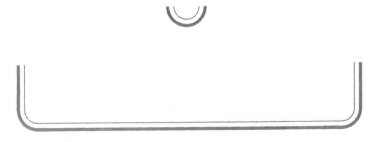

What should you tell the police officer when he stops you for passing an ambulance?

Your first mistake was paying attention to the officer and stopping, for that implied that you thought you were in the wrong. Now, your best move is to say "Excuse me, sir, the blinking lights confused me. I thought it was a school bus." This should stun the officer long enough for you to dash off and double-park somewhere. The fine for double-parking isn't too bad.

If you bid a dramatic farewell to someone at the train station, and then the train is delayed so you wait around, must you bid a second dramatic farewell?

No. Good-byes are silly enough. Doing them over adds a crowning touch of humiliation. But you can't just stroll off without saying a word when the train comes either. People find that cold. As soon as the train's arrival is announced, put your hand to your chest and gasp, "Aunt Ruthie's gold brooch! It's in my soup at the Rainbow Buffet!" Tear away, yelling as you go, "Enjoy Fort Dix. See you in a year."

Chapter 7

Health and Fitness

To spare yourself a lecture, is it permissible to lie and tell your dental hygienist you *do* floss?

There are some dental hygienists, like Miss Dancie, who derive great pleasure from marshaling you out of the dentist's chair to help you see the plaque on your teeth under the Special Light, and then to show you a poster that illustrates, stage by stage, the gum disease you will get if you don't use dental floss. The poster is not as amusing as the poster by Denise, age seven, of a big smile that says, ''President Reagan brushes three times a day!!! How about you??!!'' Tell Miss Dancie you *do* floss. Or don't tell her. You are going to get the lecture anyway.

If you smoke cigarettes and eat junk food all day, should you bother exercising?

"In the long run," said John Maynard Keynes, "we are all dead." Exercise will not change this. It will only get your body's hopes up.

> If you're expecting a very important phone call but must go out for half an hour, is it a good idea to take the phone off the hook?

A fascinating study of twins addresses this problem. Dave and Don Danner were identical twins separated at birth and never reunited. Both happened to become ill with a rare heart disease on the same day. Again coincidentally, Dave and Don decided to go to the bank before it closed, though both knew that the doctor was supposed to call shortly with the lab results. Don took the phone off the hook; Dave decided not to.

Dave's doctor called and, finding no one home, broke into Dave's house so that he could leave a message saying Dave had only twenty-four hours to live. The police arrived and threw Dave's doctor in jail. Ironically, Dave's doctor was put into the same cell as Don's doctor (even though the doctors were not twins). Don's doctor was in on charges of illegal sale of narcotics and extortion against construction companies: He had called Don, found his number busy, and thought, Oh, well, might as well use this time to make a few deals. In jail, the doctors began to talk of their respective patients, not suspecting that Dave and Don were related. Still, in a matter of minutes, it became clear that Dave had been born with Don's heart and vice versa. The governor pardoned the doctors from jail, and they rushed to the hospital to transplant Dave's heart into Don and Don's heart into Dave. The twins realized their true identities, sold their story to a major network, and went on to lead happy and full lives.

But it all could have ended tragically if Dave and Don had

different doctors. Dave and Don, like you and me, can never predict how someone will react to our taking the phone off the hook or leaving it on. Therefore, you shouldn't worry about it. Good or bad, something will happen.

Incidentally, this study also proves that environment, not heredity, determines whether you will take the phone off the hook.

Should you ask a police officer to redirect the Mummers Parade down Chestnut Street so that you can look for your contact lens on Market Street?

Yes. It is most thoughtful of you to consider redirecting the parade yourself, but without keen vision, you are likely to cause traffic congestion. When you have found your lens, the police officer can drive you to Chestnut Street; there is no reason for you to miss any more of the parade.

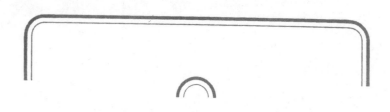

Is it okay to make up your social security number on the form at the hospital where you have been taken for emergency surgery, or should you ask the ambulance driver to take you back home to find your card?

Make it up by all means. By the time the nurse has located the person to whom the made-up number belongs, it will be too late for the doctor to give that person the operation instead of you. Even Abraham Lincoln, after he was shot and rushed to the hospital, fudged a little on the form. When they asked for his address, he tried to fit it all in, then gave up and just wrote "Gettysburg."

When should you say something to someone who puts too much salt on his or her food?

When he or she is your Siamese twin.

If someone tells you that you look great, must you return the compliment?

On the contrary. You should never speak to that person again; for like the Bible, the phrase "You look great" can be interpreted many ways. One way is "I don't know . . . you look so awful I just can't think of what to say." Similarly, when someone tells you how healthy you look, what he means is "Wow, are you ever fat." Or when someone tells you that you look well, he is thinking, "You look well for someone who is surely on death's door." Another way to put that is "You look so serious these days." Likewise:

When someone says	He is thinking
What a pretty color!	They'll be able to find you in the parking lot.
You're looking quite the sophisticate.	God, have you aged.
Those are nice shoes.	Did you join the circus?
I like your hair.	How often do you have to water it?
You look really happy.	They must have you on antidepressants now.
You're looking rested.	If I looked like you, I'd put a bullet through my head.

Chapter 8

Manners

How should you respond to someone who thanks you profusely for something you did not do?

A responsible person would say "You're welcome."

What should you do if you are introducing someone and forget his name?

If you can remember the name in Latin, use that. People are always impressed by Latin. Otherwise, use the name of the most attractive person you both know. Your friend is less likely to mind that you forgot who he was if you mistake him for, say, Warren Beatty. If the name never dawns on you, stick with Warren, and gradually, it will become an in-joke in the way that anything becomes a joke if you repeat it relentlessly over the course of a long time.

Do you have to pet other people's dogs?

Dogs may have no formal education, but they are streetsmart and can tell when someone is being patronizing. Treat a dog with dignity — shake his paw, perhaps — and he will be less likely to attack you brutally in old age when his skull presses against his brain causing him to go berserk.

How much should you tip a bad waitress?

Fifteen percent, unless the waitress is your mother, in which case tipping would be in bad taste. Instead, when you leave home for good, say at the age of nineteen or twenty-one, send your mother — and father — a nice thank-you note like the one that follows, and don't forget to check under the bed and in the shower to see that you've left nothing behind.

> *Dear Mom and Dad,*
>
> *Thank you for the lovely time I had growing up. Your warm hospitality really made me feel at home, and don't think I didn't notice, with tremendous gratitude, that my room was bigger than Lucy's.*
>
> *Home was centrally located and a great experience, especially during the teen years. Thanks again and stay well.*
>
> *Your son,*
> *George*

What should you say if you are talking to a foreigner and can't understand a word he's saying but have already asked him to repeat himself three times?

"Speak English or get out of the country" is a bit harsh. The foreigner probably wants directions, so tell him to go straight and take a left at the elevator.

How do you thank someone for a present when you have no idea what it is?

You might give the present to someone else and see what he says, but often it is better not to know. Imagine how difficult it must have been for the maiden who had to write a thank-you note to her true love for the ten lords a-leapin' that he sent.

If the cat jumps up on the kitchen table and nibbles on the chicken, can you serve the chicken to your family?

Might you instead serve the cat?

Chapter 9

Philosophy and Morality

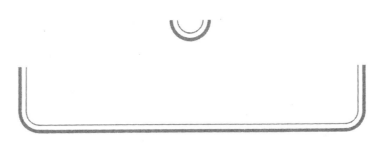

When a recipe calls for only the caps of the mushroom, what should you do with the pound of leftover stems?

Mushroom stems taste almost as good as wood chips, so your first thought might be to throw them out. But your second thought might be of the starving masses. Rather than throw out all that fresh food, you could consider making mushroom bisque. This, however, would require buying a lot of cream, and it would not ease the plight of the starving masses at all unless you open a soup kitchen. You don't have enough bowls to do that. The simplest solution is to put the stems in the refrigerator for five days and then throw them away. No one could criticize you for throwing out moldy mushroom stems.

How many dinner reservations is it ethical to make for the same night?

It is ethical to make as many dinner reservations as you like in someone else's name.

Is it all right to take an umbrella you find in the back of a taxi?

God helps those who help themselves. Take the umbrella, it will stop raining, and you can leave the umbrella in the next taxi you're in.

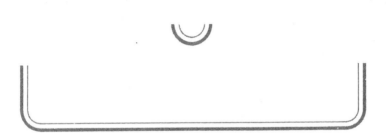

Is it okay to read someone else's mail that is sitting on the kitchen table?

Many people believe you should read only that which is written for you. Nonsense. *Road to My Heart* was written "for Debbie, who was always there with a cup of coffee," but nonetheless I, and I think thousands of others, have rightfully enjoyed the novella. Anyone who says it is wrong to read *Road to My Heart* or to read another person's mail advocates censorship. Censorship is morally reprehensible. It is almost as abhorrent as neglecting to open the letter on the table if it is sealed. There may be a notice inside saying the heat will be shut off unless payment is immediately forthcoming. Now, better rifle through the drawers to see if there's any money lying around for the heat.

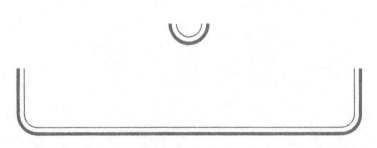

If you illegally sublet an apartment, which you are illegally subletting yourself, what can you do if your tenant decides he won't get out?

When you break the law, you can not always count on things to go your way. You can find a better place to live, though, in the *New York Review of Books* classifieds, under "Exchanges." Pick something that suits your tastes — a hacienda in Spain or a Kensington townhouse — then write to the owners offering them your illegal sublet, which you describe with allure. By the time you are settled abroad, your subletter, sublettee, and the Europeans will have become wonderful friends, united by their deep hatred of you.

Is it vain to change your first name?

No, it is stupid. Your first name is one of the few things you have in life that does not reflect your taste. It shows that your parents are tacky and credits you with rising above such roots. This does not mean that you should hang up the large needlepoint sampler of your name that your mother made for you.

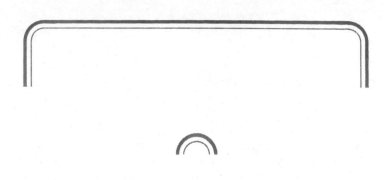

Is it permissible to take a bad photograph of yourself from someone's wallet
while he is not looking?

According to the Eskimos, your soul is trapped within that
photograph. Your soul does not belong in someone's wallet.
It belongs in your wallet, though for what purpose I do not
know. You have a right to confiscate the photograph. On closer
inspection, however, it seems the Eskimos have not carefully
thought through this soul-in-the-photograph thing. Why is it
that you can take two different pictures of the same person?
Anyway, what's the negative supposed be—the id?

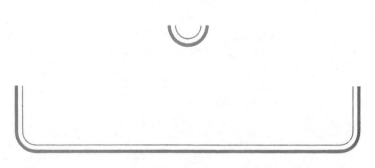

Are you a bad person if you place your box of popcorn on the floor of the theater when you leave?

On the contrary. You are a saint to have provided a convenient trash receptacle for those who sit in your seat in the shows to come. You have littered so that others do not have to; you have borne their guilt.

Should you feel guilty if you lie and say your aunt in New Hampshire just died so that you don't have to go to a baby shower, and then your aunt in New Hampshire really does die?

It's the baby's fault. Sue.

What should you do if you are sitting on a jury and can't make up your mind about the verdict because you were daydreaming about the defense attorney during most of the trial?

Perjury is bad but embarrassment is worse. Don't admit under any circumstances that you don't have a clue to what has been going on for the last two weeks. In *Perry Mason*, the one who did it is the one introduced before the first commercial, who has no fathomable motive for committing the crime. With minor adjustment, this mode of deduction can be applied to your case, too.

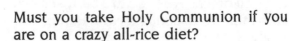

Must you take Holy Communion if you are on a crazy all-rice diet?

To refuse might be to insult someone you can't afford to insult. Besides, in heaven you are judged by your soul, and the fatter the better.

How can you explain human suffering if there is a God?

Shouldn't God be the one explaining?

01048086
ISBN 0-395-38465-6